AROUND
LOUTH
A SECOND SELECTION

BRITAIN
IN OLD PHOTOGRAPHS

Around
LOUTH
A Second Selection

David Cuppleditch

SUTTON PUBLISHING

Sutton Publishing Limited
Phoenix Mill · Thrupp · Stroud
Gloucestershire · GL5 2BU

First published 2002

This edition first published 2003

Copyright © David Cuppleditch, 2002

Title page photograph: The Priory,
Eastgate, Louth.

British Library Cataloguing in Publication Data
A catalogue record for this book is available from the
British Library.

ISBN 0-7509-3533-2

Typeset in 10.5/13.5 Photina.
Typesetting and origination by
Sutton Publishing Limited.
Printed and bound in England by
J.H. Haynes & Co. Ltd, Sparkford.

Undoubtedly the oldest newspaper in Lincolnshire was the *Lincoln, Rutland and Stamford Mercury*, which began life around 1695. A plethora of newspaper imprints flooded the market place in Victorian times, including the *Lincolnshire Free Press* (1847), *Market Rasen Monitor* (1856), *Lincolnshire Times* (1857), *Horncastle News* (1885) and the *Lincolnshire Echo* (1893). Brodgen's *The Louth Monthly Record and Local Advertiser* made its first appearance in March 1869, while the *Louth Times* (later called *Louth Times and Mablethorpe and Sutton Advertiser*) was first published in 1872 by Mr Edward Ruscoe of 91 Eastgate.

CONTENTS

The crowning glory of Louth is the magnificent spire of St James's parish church (295ft high), here seen floodlit. It is the tallest parish church spire in England.

INTRODUCTION

'To my Friends, both in the town and out of it – friends far and near – these verses and notes on "Loyal Little Louth" are dedicated with a kind good will.'

So wrote W.T. Klime, in his introduction to the now collectable volume of poems entitled *Louth: a souvenir of the writer's birthplace*, printed by W.A. Larder of the Advertiser Office, Market Place. The sentiment applies equally well today. In 1988 Kate Stockdale wrote to me, 'We may have met in our rock 'n' roll days. In 1958 I was sixteen and went to all the dances I was allowed. I belonged to Trinity Youth Club and went to dances at the Town Hall and the Pavilion. Previous to rock 'n' roll I was a keen old tyme dancer at the Liberal Club on a Friday night. I'm afraid I was also one of the "hooligans" who danced in the aisles when "Rock Around the Clock" was first shown at the Playhouse Cinema. Wasn't it a wonderful time to be a teenager?' As I recall, the dances in the Town Hall came to a stop when someone fell over the balcony (or was pushed) and died!

Louth has enjoyed so many colourful characters over the years it is difficult to know where to begin. John Jackson established his printing and bookselling business in the Market Place in Louth in 1797. He was a contemporary of Robert Sheardown who in 1788, set up the first printing press in Louth. It was Jackson who agreed to the risky undertaking of publishing *Poems by Two Brothers* in 1827, the year which also saw the first published work of Alfred Lord Tennyson. The Bard was later to pen his classic, 'Charge of the Light Brigade', with the immortal lines:

Their's not to make reply,
Their's not to reason why,
Their's but to do and die. . .

which is just as relevant to present-day England as it was in the nineteenth century.

Another wonderful character was Sir John Fox, known locally as Major John St Vigor-Fox, High Steward of Louth for many years until his resignation in 1960. He died at Pilton in Somerset in 1968 at the grand old age of ninety. In his day, he was a great follower of foxhounds, and in 1913 was the joint master with Sir Montague Cholmley of the Burton Hunt. Always immaculately turned out, he was also a keen amateur cricketer and kept wicket despite the terrible leg wounds he incurred in the First World War. Many people of the older generation can remember his splendid open-top green Bentley racing car as he drove into Louth to attend civic duties. He married twice, the first time in 1902 to Miss Esther Waldo Sibthorp of Canwick Hall, Lincoln, and the second time to Sylvia Sutton of Thetford. All that remains of his country pile, Girsby Manor, is a pair of sculpted foxes.

Then there was Captain Webb, who captained Louth cricket team for many years and who was friendly with the great English batsman Jack Hobbs. Both of Captain Webb's sons boarded at Lincoln School on Wragby Road, where Jack Hobbs was persuaded to play twice! On each occasion the modest and talented batsman gave a superb account of himself. Captain Webb was the local Conservative agent who lived opposite Holy Trinity church. Both his sons joined the army.

Louth has traditionally been a peaceful town – only five murders over the past hundred years – and it has always been a relatively safe place to bring up children. But there have been some bizarre events, such as the story that appeared on 19 March 1993 when a man's body was found in a Louth flat, six weeks after he had died. Nigel Brown was discovered in Newbridge Court after complaints from neighbours about a strong smell. His partner, Nora Prendergast, had panicked and covered him in a shroud, keeping the corpse in a corner of the room. She was later counselled by Social Services. This story is matched by that of the British Schools at Louth in 1728. The British schoolroom adjoined the stables and the effluvia from the animals entered the room through cracks in the walls. The indignation of the schoolmaster may be imagined when the owner of the stable complained that the noise made by the children disturbed the horses!

The first Englishman to fly in space, Dr Michael Foale, was born in Louth and the first English woman to sit in Parliament, Margaret Wintringham (Nancy Astor was American), represented Louth. It is these astonishing facts to which Louth can lay claim, rather than the flippant comment derived from Louth's bulging retirement sector prompting the remark that Louth is the equivalent of God's waiting room. The first Duchess of Marlborough, Sarah Jennings, responsible for the famous Churchill line, was born at Burwell Park (now demolished) and the controversial novelist and campaigner for authors' rights, Brigid Brophy, died in Fir Close Nursing Home in 1995. Barbara Dickson, the singer now turned actress, can often be seen shopping in Louth, while a host of TV personalities drift in and out of Louth on a regular basis. Jim Broadbent, the actor who has a holiday cottage at Little Carlton, has been joined by Patrick Mower, currently starring in *Emmerdale*. There are memories here of Liza Goddard who rented the Old Mill at Legbourne with her then husband Colin Baker, back in the late '60s and early '70s, when many celebrities could be seen popping into 'The Splash' (The Royal Oak).

But it is the buildings that have changed so much. Gone is the distinctive Corn Exchange frontage and the United Free Methodist Chapel on Eastgate, which resembled a huge Greek temple. The gasometers off Monks Dyke Road have been removed but the Malt Kiln still survives as a permanent eyesore and in the postwar period Louth has seen the erection of scores of bungalows. But covering all these changes has been the eagle eye of generations of photographers, whose work has often been maligned or merely forgotten. The selection of their work shown here, most of which has not been published before, bears witness to their unfailing tenacity.

David Cuppleditch
November 2001

1

Old Louth

1896. Just off the bridal path at Abbey Park and Eastfield Road, on the way to Cowslip Lane and Keddington church, this delightful photograph was taken by Joseph Matthews. It depicts his wife Florence (under the umbrella), his daughter, son Harold and their friends.

1870. In the field behind Ivy Bank on Upgate, young and impressionable Victorian girls were encouraged to play badminton and croquet as part of their moral upbringing. The fresh air was good for their health and the games stopped them thinking about other things – notably boys!

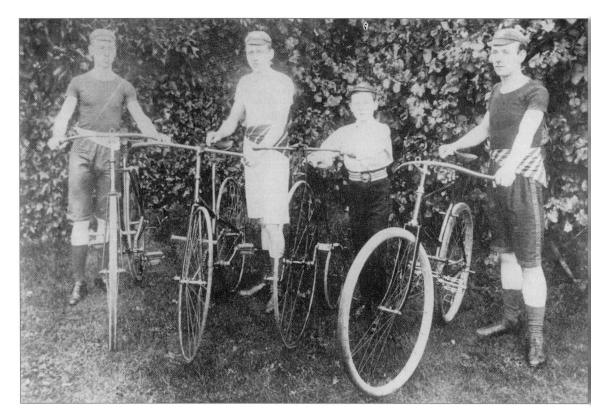

Much emphasis was put on physical exercise in this era. Apart from walking, the other popular pastime was cycling. Here we see a group of Louth wheelers, comprising the Richardson family. J.P. Hodgson of 27 and 29 Mercer Row sold a vast array of bicycles, including the Luda cycle, built to order, with Eadie or BSA fittings, from £6 10s. Accessories such as lamps, bells, carriers and capes were also available.

As bicycles became more streamlined, the old gas lamps were replaced by dynamo battery lighting. This young boy is showing off his brand new cycle outside 97 Newmarket.

1895. The Blue Stone Inn, the legendary
Upgate pub, named after the blue stone
which once stood in Upgate and which
can be found today outside Louth
museum.

1900. At the turn of the century the
cattle market was a hive of activity.
Farmers came from far and near to trade
and local traders took advantage of their
custom. These were the sheep pens at a
time when the market was divided into
three sections, for sheep, cattle and pigs.

Many firms have come and gone in Louth. This was the Victorian premises of George Tidman in Eastgate, booksellers, printers and stationers. Tidman's also dealt in patent medicines and paper hangings.

Fell's drapery store (formerly Burton & Son) at 49 Eastgate.

Traditionally Louth has always produced fine butchers. This was the Louth Meat Company's shop at 103 Eastgate, on the site of the present Pridmore Men's Clothing premises.

The most prestigious private residence in the Louth area is the Elizabethan Thorpe Hall, built in 1584 by Sir John Bolle. Several important Louth families have lived here, including John Fytche and Captain Julius Tennyson (nephew of the Poet Laureate). In 1906 Captain Langton Brackenbury MP bought the property, and from 1938 to 1953 Geoffrey Harmsworth, Director of *The Field* magazine, lived here. In the twentieth century the Hall passed to Sir John and Lady Marsden, Lady Evelyn Patrick, Nick Shailer and the present owners, Mr and Mrs Robin Mitchell. This photograph, *c.* 1865, was taken by Plumtree.

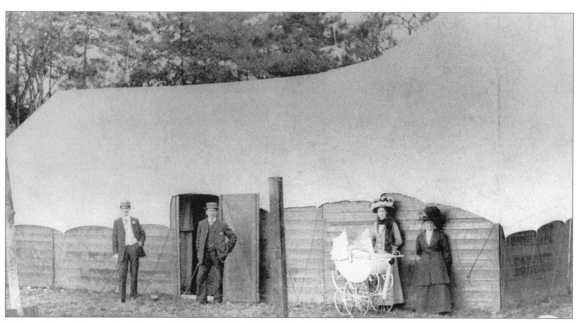

A travelling cinema in Westgate fields. Before Mr Roberts purchased the Electric Light Cinema in Eastgate he erected this semi-permanent construction to show the latest in moving pictures.

Above: Originally there were three fulling mills in Louth (for fulling and milling woollen cloth). This one, situated in Shepebridge Lane, Westgate, was known as the Thorpe Hall Mill. Subsequently it became a paper mill, then a corn mill, and finally a trout farm before becoming a housing complex known as Troutbeck.

A view of Thorpe Hall Mill taken from Mill Bridge. Incidentally, the bridge, known simply as Mill Bridge, was painted by Thomas Wilkinson Wallis and now hangs as part of his collection of Louth bridges in the Mayor's parlour.

At 104 Eastgate was the Leeds & Leicester Boot Company Limited, with its splendid array of footwear. Their main rivals were Stead and Simpson of 26 Market Place and perhaps Smith's of 8 Mercer Row (formerly in Upgate). These premises are currently occupied by Marris Carpets.

View from the corner of Eastgate and Burnt Hill Lane. The Leeds & Leicester Boot Company can be seen (five shops along from the old Jolly Sailor pub) on the right.

Queen Street. Many of the buildings on the right have since been demolished. In the foreground is T.H. Wyer's of Burnthill Lane and Queen Street. Wyer's were glaziers and gas fitters and sold an assortment of acetylene plants, electric bells, burners and gas mantles.

Eastgate looking back towards St James's Church and showing Cheetham's store on the right (next to Swaby butcher's). This was to become the Palace cinema before it was converted to a Fine Fare supermarket and, most recently, a Wilkinson's (Wilko's) hardware department store.

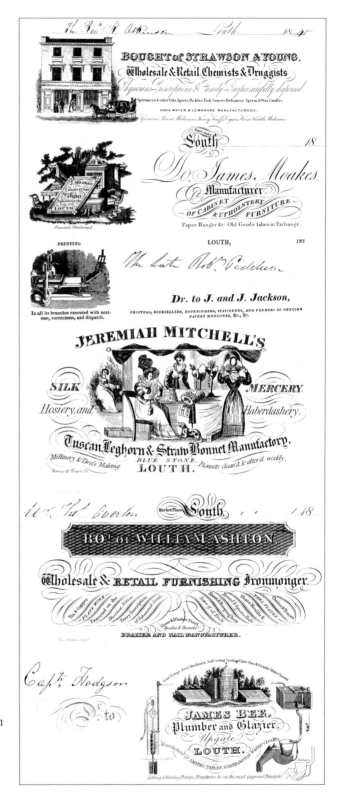

Before the advent of photography, many firms relied on illustrators. This is a selection of old Louth businesses' billheads, each of which had its own logo for advertising purposes.

1899. Christopher Thomas Robinson, nurseryman, was the son of William Robinson who started Robinson's fruit and vegetable business in 1834. Robinson's fruit shop still operates successfully at 125 Eastgate. He was photographed by Jancowski.

1900. The young girl standing in the gateway of her parents' house at the top end of Lee Street, opposite the cattle market, is Miss Edna Broadley. She was the sister of Herbert Broadley, later Sir Herbert Broadley. Their father was a wheelwright, joiner, painter, undertaker and zealous Baptist. The house has long been demolished but the surname survives in Broadley Crescent.

Plumtree was the forerunner of Arthur James, photographer. This was a *carte de visite* typical of his work, possibly showing a Victorian brother and sister or a young man and his wife. Even the humblest of families queued up to have their photograph taken.

1905. Before the First World War many Louth families grew their own vegetables and were thus self-sufficient. This photograph of Janet Boswell was taken in the garden outside 191 Newmarket (now 167 Newmarket). She was born in 1896 and died at the age of nineteen.

This was the Ladies and Gentlemen's cricket match played at the turn of the century.

'Uncle Nell', part of the Norfolk family who owned Norfolk House (now Douglas Electronics) photographed by J. Willey of Aswell Lane. This was probably Richard Norfolk (1849–1922). The chair in this photograph (a studio prop) appears in many of Willey's *carte de viste* and cabinet portraits.

'Aunt Hyde', also photographed by J. Willey. Norfolk House included four cottages (known as Norfolk Row) which ran alongside the main house, and further dwellings in Norfolk Terrace.

The proclamation of Edward VII as King on 29 January 1901 saw crowds of people in the Market Place listening to Mayor Hurd Hickling's address.

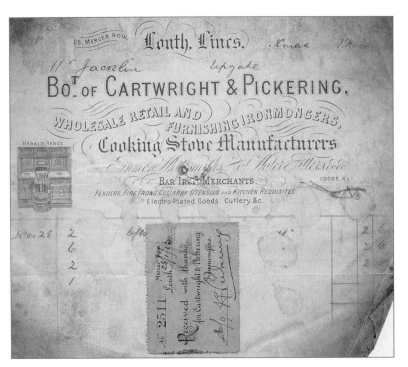

1902. Cartwright & Pickering was one of the many established firms that disappeared in the twentieth century. In 1902 they were based at 26 Mercer Row and when they finally closed their doors in about 1995/6 they were situated in Eastgate.

1902. The staff of Golding's printing shop on their works outing. These special holidays were usually held in the summer months, with this particular one venturing as far afield as the New Inn, Saltfleet.

1902. When Lieutenant John Frederic Eve died in 1902, at the relatively young age of forty, he was given a military funeral in Louth. A great many people turned out to pay their last respects and shops closed for the day to mark this sad occasion (note the drawn wooden shutters). J.F. Eve, the son of John Bowmar Eve, was the last Eve in the firm of Eve and Ranshaw.

1903. On 11 June the Great Louth Walking Match gathered for the start in Eastgate. There were forty-six contestants.

1903. The winner of the match was Harry Coppin, seen here with his medals (see also page 35). He owned Coppin's Bazaar (on the site of today's Falkner's electricians).

1907. In this year the Jackson family erected an iron bridge on Grimsby Road. Matthew Jackson, corn merchant, purchased land on the opposite side of the Grimsby Road for use as a garden. The bridge provided access.

1907. The area known as Hubbard's Valley was donated in August 1907 to the good citizens of Louth for recreational purposes. Canon A.S. Wilde handed over the deeds and practically the entire population of the town turned out to witness the event. Hubbard's Valley was named after Alexander Hubbard, who died at Hallington in 1793.

1910. View of Hubbard's Hills showing the Fowleresque Victorian water pump with its distinctive chimney in the background. The photograph was probably taken by Nainby of Alford.

1908. An unsuccessful attempt at studio portraiture: the sitter has moved at just the wrong moment! The photographer did not leave his imprint.

An advert in the *Louth and Lincolnshire Advertiser* of 13 June 1908 claimed that A. James was 'the oldest established photographer in Louth'. Out of the thousands of portraits that Arthur James took, this particular study fascinates the author: it looks as if the attractive young lady has had her head oddly transposed on to the negative.

1908. On Saturday 31 October an advert appeared in the *Louth and North Lincolnshire News* (known locally as the *Louth Times*) and the *Mablethorpe and Sutton-on-Sea Advertiser* for Henry Rose's gramophones at 120 Eastgate. This should not be confused with Jesse Hall's music shop at 137 Eastgate.

1909. Mawer Brothers' carpentry workshop. Prior to the First World War Mawer Brothers had as many as sixty craftsmen carpenters on their books. Their premises off Kidgate occupied what is now known as the Woolmart, Kai's Bar and the group of newly built shops just opposite.

1910. The Masons' Arms bus, photographed here in Hubbard's Hills, was the equivalent of Thorn's cabs. It carried customers to and from Louth station and to any other venue they wished to visit. But its life was to be brief because the Masons' Arms would buy a fleet of motorised horseless carriages just after the First World War.

1910. Opposition to sectarian education mounted in the early twentieth century. Louth Borough elders imposed fines on chapel schools, which often had to auction their contents to pay the fines. This august body included F.S. Riggall, Mrs Riggall, James Lill, J.W. Dennis and auctioneer Mr Vere.

1911. Following in the footsteps of Lord Baden-Powell, who visited Louth twice, a group of Louth Boy Scouts juggle with billycans at their Easter Camp.

Captain Langton Brackenbury stood briefly as
MP for Louth in 1910 but was toppled by the
Liberal Timothy Davies. After the First World
War he campaigned again, taking the unusual
measure of sending his family out to lobby on
his behalf.

1910. On the corner of South Terrace and
Newmarket stood 97 Newmarket (currently 135)
with its iron railings, Edwardian drapes and
monkey-puzzle tree.

1912. This laundry was situated between Irish Hill and Love Lane. Despite using the dolly tub, C.G. Smith's carbolic soap, an old-fashioned mangle and steam irons, the washing was always clean and crisply starched. Riverdale (built in 1911) on the corner of Crowtree Lane and Love Lane, is just visible in the background.

1912. Louth Dye Works and Steam Laundry. The young gentleman standing in the third row (extreme left) is Alexander McIntyre. He was born in Perth in 1884 and married Miss Dobbs in Louth in 1908. The gentleman with the moustache in the row behind him, also extreme left, is Frederick William Dobbs (born 1860).

1914. Harry Coppin shows off his new Lincoln Elk motorcycle. This was made by Kirby and Edwards of Broadgate, Lincoln. Minerva motorcycles had a similar design.

914. This photograph of a group of shoeing smiths completing their RSS and AFCL certificates, was taken n August at Dunkin's forge, Eve Street. Captain Routledge (centre) was a surgeon in the Army Veterinary Corps (mentioned in despatches). He died in 1918 and is buried in Louth Cemetery.

1915. Captains Oscar Dixon and Huskinson photographed at Luton. During service with the 5th Lincolns Oscar Dixon was wounded on 30 May when a stray bullet ricocheted from a private's wrist watch and embedded itself into his arm and shoulder. He brought the 'Monchy' bell back to Louth, which had been captured by 'A' Coy 5th Lincolns on 18 October 1916 on a raid at Monchy au Bois from the famous German 180th Regiment who had defended Thiepval.

2

Between the Wars

1919. Motorised taxis were now being used to ferry passengers to and from Louth station.
Here we see John Evarson (taxi driver) still dressed in military uniform. He worked for
H. Dawes, using the number-plate GY 1091.

1918. Dr W.R. Higgins (1878–1930) was responsible for founding an ex-servicemen's club in Louth after the First World War, where he was affectionately known as Dr Willie. Dr William Robert Higgins MA, MD, FRCS, died in the Shaftesbury Hotel, Liverpool, after a holiday cruise.

1922. The model for the statue on Louth's famous War Memorial, pictured here with puttees and bayonet.

1919. To commemorate the peace of 1919 every child in Louth was given a medal. This was Newmarket Girls School.

1919. This band of banjos and fiddles provided a little light relief after the dismal war years. The photograph was probably taken in the grounds of the Cedars.

1919. At the junction of Mercer Row and Upgate was the Louth Leather Company, with Campion's next door. Later this became the Lincolnshire Gun Shop and, latterly, an Indian restaurant.

Looking down the Grimsby Road towards Bridge Street was Espin's Garage. The pavement was of the brick variety – the same type of brick that was used in Louth cattle market and elsewhere in Louth.

Howard's Yard (off Upgate). The boss, Hamish Hodgson, is on the far right, wearing the trilby hat. Third from left is Charles Robinson.

1920. The football team of King Edward VI Grammar School for Boys. The captain, Chris Robinson (1901–91), is seated, holding the ball. Crowtree Lane and the Sycamores are visible in the background.

1920. Photographically the best-recorded event in Louth's long and illustrious history was also its most tragic – the Louth flood. A memorial in the cemetery plays tribute to those who lost their lives, and here we see some of the bereaved on their way to the cemetery. Canon Lenton officiated. For further reading see *The Louth Flood* by D. Robinson.

Ramsgate House, 1920. In the aftermath of the Louth flood many buildings had to be propped up with scaffolding. This house in Ramsgate was eventually demolished. Eric Woods, the Louth photographer, lived here.

1920. Hurst's Yard at the Riverhead was also badly damaged. Individual bricks were collected after the flood and placed in piles for reuse, as in the picture below.

This unusual Victorian greenhouse in Enginegate (now called Broadbank) was wrecked.

1922. Louth War Memorial was unveiled in this year under the auspices of Alderman Lacey and Sydney Jackson – one Mayor of Louth at the time of its conception, the other at the time of its unveiling. Lacey Gardens was named after Alderman Lacey, of Lacey and Greaves, printers and stationers. Sydney Jackson had an unfortunate death after choking on a fish bone. He had just visited the dentist's too!

1922. The War Memorial was built by Harrison stonemasons to the design of Harold Hall, but the most interesting feature of this photograph is the view of Clare's photographer's (next to the Eastgate chapel), which has since been demolished to make way for public conveniences.

1923. Staff from F. Grounsell's Northgate Iron Works in a state-of-the-art charabanc, ready for their works outing. Photographed outside the Orme Almshouses on the corner of Eastgate and Ramsgate.

The Louth canal finally closed its waterways to traffic in 1924. It was built in 1767 at a cost of £28,000 but took such a pounding in the 1920 flood that it could no longer operate profitably.

1924. Prior to the opening of Bateson's Baths (the swimming pool in Maiden Row), swimming events were held in the only other available public place – at the Riverhead. Note the contrast between people dressed in bathing costumes standing next to fully suited gentlemen with trilbies, bow ties and cloth caps.

Bateson's Baths opened in Maiden Row (later Church Street) in 1924. It was served by a copious supply of cold spring water from Aswell Springs, which flowed into Monks Dyke.

1924. Apart from the public baths and the Riverhead, the only other place to enjoy the pleasures of a quick dip was the Grammar School's own pool.

1924. A group of Grammar School girls photographed outside the Limes. The class of IIA. Back row, left to right: Annie Lancaster, -?-, Joan Brittle, Beryl Tommy, Cathlene Hoe, Margaret Tucker. Middle row: Mary Hall, Stoven ?, Betty Binnington, Kinwyn Smith, ? Jarvis. Bottom row: Beatrice Baker, Pamela Dobson, Madge Parrinder, Irene Brown and Mary Trafford.

The start of the
1924 Louth and
District Hospital Cup
Final. All profits
went to Crowtree
Lane Hospital.

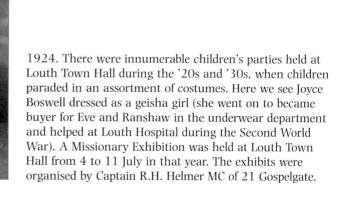

1924. There were innumerable children's parties held at
Louth Town Hall during the '20s and '30s, when children
paraded in an assortment of costumes. Here we see Joyce
Boswell dressed as a geisha girl (she went on to became
buyer for Eve and Ranshaw in the underwear department
and helped at Louth Hospital during the Second World
War). A Missionary Exhibition was held at Louth Town
Hall from 4 to 11 July in that year. The exhibits were
organised by Captain R.H. Helmer MC of 21 Gospelgate.

King Edward VIII Grammar School for Girls, 1925, when the fearsome Miss Nalder (third row, centre) was Headmistress. To her right are Miss Knight, Miss Barton-Jones, Miss Curtis, Miss Barker, Miss Phillips and Miss Ingoldby. To her left are Miss Patchell, Miss Davies and Miss Stevens. In the front row is a young Ken Drinkell (eighth from left) and Mick Lill (fifth from right).

A march past of Girl Guides in Mercer Row. Mr and Mrs Smith watch the procession from their first-floor window.

Mrs Oscar Dixon addressing a group of Girl Guides at Kenwick Hall in 1933. On her right is Mrs Heneage (wife of the MP) and on her left is Mrs Tennyson D'Eyncourt of Tealby Manor. The Guides are, from left to right, Catherine Poole, Vivien Bury, Evelyn Smith and Doris Stamper.

1926. Staff of the glove factory, photographed at the Riverhead in February. The glove factory in Thames Street was owned by Partridge and Co. of Leicester. In the front row, fourth from left, is Ivy Atkins. This factory was still operational in the '50s, although by then the ownership had transferred to Messrs Allen, Bastick and Billson.

1930. From 1925 to the Second World War Louth enjoyed a unique selection of operatic productions. One of Louth's best-loved characters, Margaret Godsmark, appeared as Dolores in the Louth amateur production of *Floradora*.

No. 38 Newmarket (now No. 40) is pretty much the same as it is today.

Right: Also photographed was Sam Stones, blacksmith of Saltfleetby. He is shown here holding young Margaret Boswell, in the backyard of 38 Newmarket.

At the back of the house this makeshift hessian gazebo was erected to protect its occupants from excessive heat and sunburn. Frank Boswell (far left) and his wife Gladys (third from left) rigged up the shelter.

1927. On 21 July Prime Minister Stanley Baldwin arrived in Louth en route to Heneage Hall, Hainton, as the guest of Lord Heneage. Major Vigor-Fox (High Steward) and Colonel A. Heneage MP were there to meet Mr and Mr Baldwin at Louth railway station.

1928. With the advent of 'the talkies', a whole new dimension came to the screen that would revolutionise entertainment. Here we see the owners and staff of the Palace cinema. Back row, left to right: Tom Baker, Ivy Blow, Reg Bateson, Ivy Bateson and Harry Kirk. Front row: Ted Goodwin, Mary Ingleton, Ernie Roberts, Martha Roberts, Graham Ingleton and Denis Ingleton.

1927. Princess Helena's visit to open the extension of Crowtree Lane Hospital led to an overnight stay at Little Grimsby Hall – the home of Margaret Winteringham.

THE PRINCESS AT GRIMSBY HALL.

With the gracious permission of Her Highness this photograph was taken exclusively for the "Louth Standard" before she left Little Grimsby Hall for the Hospital.

1927. During Princess Helena's visit to Louth, the Revd W.A. Hind (vicar of Holy Trinity) read passages from St Mark's gospel as a reminder of Christ's healing ministry and his love of children.

1928. The Market Place.

1928. Every year there was a football match to raise money for the local hospital in Crowtree Lane. This match between Frodingham Athletic and Louth Town took place on 25 August. On the left is G. Kirby (in white), Louth's left-back, while in the centre is Parrot (partly obscured by the Frodingham player heading the ball).

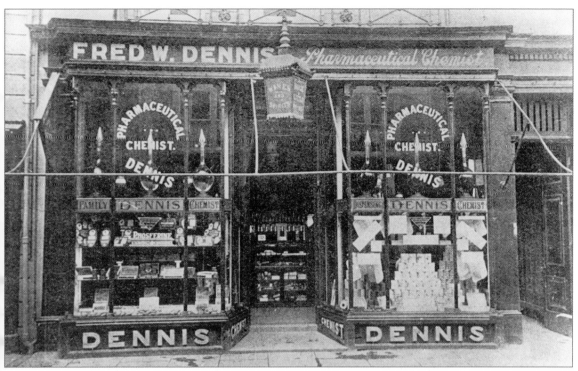

Dennis's Lincolnshire pig powders were famous throughout the county. Established before 1864 the firm was still going strong in the 1950s.

1930. At the ox roasting that took place at the Cedars, St Mary's Lane, there were many willing hands to help turn the spit. Fred Tyler, in the chef's uniform, came up to Louth from Stratford-upon-Avon to take charge of the ceremony.

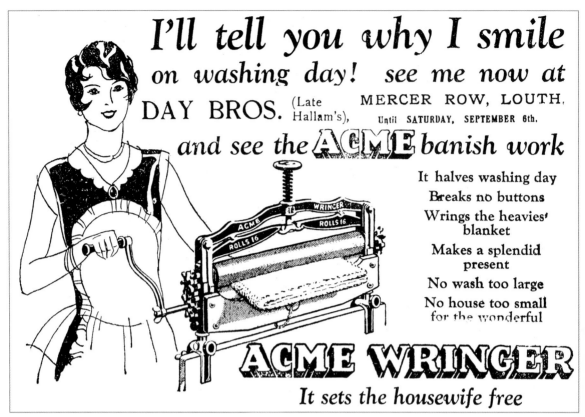

The *Louth and North Lincolnshire Advertiser*, Saturday 30 August 1930, contained this advert for the ACME Wringer. As the slogan said, 'It sets the housewife free'.

1931. Hubbard's Hills proved to be the perfect setting for a Sunday walk after church. Here is Marian Howe (wife of the Louth photographer, Les Howe) with her two sons, Brian (left) and Geoffrey (right), going over the stepping stones.

1932. The by-election of this year saw the Conservative candidate Colonel A. Heneage, elected yet again as MP for Louth. He was MP from 1924–45.

1932. This was Louth National football club photographed at the London Road sports ground in front of the old wooden stand. D. Enderby is seated in front on the left of the picture, while Arthur Price is standing fourth from right.

1932. Louth Frontiersmen on the march. The tall figure is Mr Jane.

A touch of the Far East came to Louth in 1933 when the Louth Operatic Society produced *San Toy* at the Playhouse. Operatic productions at the Playhouse were greatly encouraged by Bert Hallam. They became a fixed date in the Ludensian calendar. Photograph of the cast: Chris Robinson, Jimmy Wilson, Arthur Price and Mrs Graham.

This was the National (Nats) Football team (not to be confused with the Louth Swifts) of 1934/35 season. Back row, left to right: -?-, Hand, Grant, Foreman, Newby, -?-, Yarker. Centre row: Richardson, Rolston, Maslin, Beverley, Hollingsworth, Harboard, Horsewood. Front row: Sharpley, -?-, Vamplew, Nicholson and Harrison.

1934. Louth also had its own rugby team, pictured here with S. Grant (captain), who later became one of Louth's leading solicitors. Arthur Price is seated on his left.

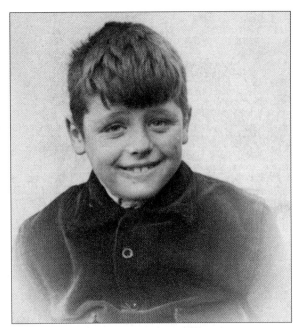

1934. John Bryan Coppin, born 17 March at Louth and District Hospital, Crowtree Lane, contracted many of the illnesses common to boys of the 1930s: whooping cough, measles, chickenpox and mumps.

1934. Of course Louth had its own natural beauty spot in Hubbard's Hills. From left to right: Ethel Morris, Gladys Boswell, Chum (the dog), Miss Robinson senior and Miss Robinson junior (the music teacher).

1934. The Louth Ramblers, founded by Mr D. Enderby (standing, left), flourished in the '30s and '40s. This enthusiastic group went rambling all over the country.

1934. Apart from Hubbard's Hills, the other great attraction in the Louth area was the spectacular Italian Gardens of Walmsgate Hall, frequently opened to the public.

The figure just visible in the distance is Gladys Boswell. The old Hall in the background (the former home of the Dallas Yorkes) was sadly demolished in 1958.

1935. The Silver Jubilee of George V and Mary celebrated in Louth as the town clerk H.E. Roberts read out a congratulatory address. The Mayor was Alderman A.E. Maxey and joint secretaries were Mr A.J. Dales and Mr Maurice Dales. The tall gentleman at the back of the group is Mr Jane, while Canon Burton is on the far left in front of Mr Street (the elderly gentleman with beard). The formidable Mrs Maxey, wife of the Mayor, is standing on the far right. H.E. Roberts came to Louth in 1910 to manage Falkners solicitors and became a partner in the firm in 1911. He was Town Clerk from 1936 to 1943.

1935. Baildom's furniture shop at 125 Eastgate, decorated for the Silver Jubilee celebrations. The name continued with Mr H.A. (Jimmy) Baildom, who was a Louth character in his own right.

Looking up from the Shambles to the Market Place.

Left: 1936. In the days when the Lincolnshire Show travelled round the county, Louth was a favourite venue. The town was decorated to welcome the 1936 Show. This was Day's ironmongery business in Mercer Row (currently Spencer's newsagents and bookshop) undergoing a facelift for the event (see page 26).

1936. The Liberal 'A' Billiard Team League Champions. Back row, left to right: F.S. Rignall, C. Walton, S. Hibbert, O. Goy, F. Parker. Front row: W.H. Smith, H. Coppin and H. Potts.

1936. In this photograph Herbert Coppin (Honorary Secretary of Louth Liberal Club) is demonstrating the art. Both billiards and snooker were popular pastimes between the wars and continued in the Old Liberal Club and the Reindeer.

1937. The White Horse Tennis Club. Included in the group are Maurice Mills, Mrs Stephenson, Mrs Knight and Miss Boswell sitting in the front. There were three grass courts for lawn tennis at the rear of the White Horse pub on Newmarket.

1936. The heartthrob of Louth, John Harrison, as he appeared as Jim Kenyon in the 1936 Louth Operatic Society's version of *Rose Marie*.

1937. Steeplejack Sydney Fawcett, photographed on the top of the spire, 25 June, during the renovation of St James's Church.

1937. To help the 'Save the Spire' effort a production of *Trial by Jury* was performed at Louth Town Hall. Pictured here are the Bride and Bridesmaids from the 1 May production. Back row, left to right: Olive Wells, Barbara Burton, Mary Carter White and Gwen Price. Front row: Vera Beckett, Kathleen Bosnell, Vera Gibbons, Jessie Hubbard and Ida Stainton.

1938. The start of the first heat of the 20-mile TT event in August at Cadwell Park. The Cadwell story started back in 1926 when Mansfield Wilkinson bought the Cadwell estate. His son Charles Wilkinson turned it into the well-known international circuit of today, with the first race meeting taking place on 24 June 1934. Over the years Jackie Beeton, Jack Surtees, Roger Marshall and Agostini have ridden on this famous motor cycle track.

One of its early stars was the winner of the Junior TT race on the Isle of Man in 1936, Freddie Frith. Although a Grimsby man by birth, he retired to Louth and died at home in St Mary's Park.

1939. Before the days of TV people had to make their own entertainment. The Christmas panto was one of the highlights of the year. Shown here are the pupils of King Edward VI Grammar School, supported by family and friends.

1939. One of Louth's most prestigious firms was Strawson's. Some of their famous products included Strawson's Christmas Pudding, Raspberry Jam, Superior Mincemeat, Butterscotch, Golden Mint Humbugs, Marmalade, Cut Mixed Peel and Glacé Cherries.

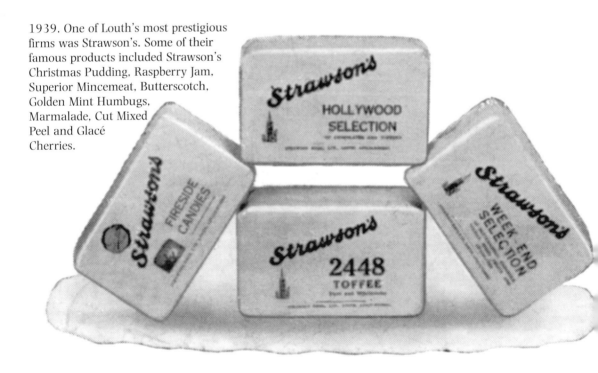

3

To the Sixties

1941. The saxophonist Basil Lock, from the group *Rhythm Racketeers*, pictured here in Louth Town Hall. He enlisted with the RAF and eventually became Air Vice-Marshal. One of his tasks was to teach the Duke of Edinburgh to fly!

1942. A tug of war conducted by the Home Guard at the 'Butts'. Jim Odlin is in the foreground.

1945. The original Kenwick Hall, home of Lieutenant Colonel Oscar Dixon, was condemned after bombs dropped close by and made the structure unsafe. It was eventually demolished and the new Kenwick Hall built on the same site. Note the unusual circular sun dial (on the plinth in the garden), which Diana Dixon transferred to St Mary's Lane when she had sold Kenwick Hall.

A winter view from the drawing-room at Kenwick Hall looking over what is part of the present golf course.

1947. During the war years the winters were bitterly cold, but the winter of 1947 took the biscuit. Snowdrifts on the Grimsby Road reached as high as the telegraph poles. And after the snow came the big freeze. This was the Louth–Grimsby railway line at the junction of Keddington Road (only the signal-box remains).

Louth's busy Market Place, photographed (above) in the 1950s. Gone is the cone-shaped water-pump, which had stood here for years. It has been replaced by a telephone kiosk. Compare this photograph with the postcard below, *c.* 1910, in which the original gas lamp, water-pump and the scissor-grinder's wheel are all clearly visible.

1950. View over Newbridge Hill looking towards Ramsgate. The two gas holders stand out clearly beyond the East Lincs. Motor Company Garage. Also visible is the old Prince of Wales pub.

1950. Work in progress: erection of the malt kiln, next to the railway station. Newbridge Hill is on the right. The old malt kiln was bombed by incendiaries on 5 December 1940.

1950. View from the Market Place towards the Fish Shambles, with Eve and Ranshaw's on the left and Godsmark's emporium on the right. The author's recollection of Godsmark's is of a series of overhead wires rather like tram cables which took customers' money in small wooden tubes to a central cashier. It seemed to work but may have caused problems for unusually tall people.

1951. After the war more emphasis was given to the state of Britain's roads. This was the A16 being widened and improved to cope with increased levels of traffic at Swaby.

In Victoria Road the old corporation steamroller was put through its paces by Fred Towle (known locally as Roller-Towl) with a fresh coat of tarmacadam. The Fowler steamroller's maximum speed was 4 miles per hour!

1952. Staff outings were still photographed in the '50s. Here we see the staff of Palmer Construction of Ramsgate on a works party to Chatsworth House, Derbyshire, with the boss, Mr Lonsdale (centre), and the architect, Mr Warren Neal, far left. Palmer Construction was situated opposite Uncle Tom's Cabin on the site of the old Labour Exchange.

1953. To mark the Coronation of Elizabeth II, the Palace cinema (now Wilko's) was decorated with bunting and Union Jacks. The east coast floods of 1953 had grabbed the headlines on the newsreels in February.

1953. There were also street parties for children. This one was held in Jubilee Crescent, where trestle tables were set up and children enjoyed sandwiches, jelly and lashings of ginger beer. It is worth noting how many of the mothers are still wearing their pinnies. Anyone with a television set was inundated with friends they never thought they had.

1954. Former guardsman Steve Lee (centre), bowling for charity at Elkington Hall. The selection of cars parked in the background is interesting in view of the fact that there were so few cars in Louth in the '50s.

1954. A Standard motor car parked outside Lound Hill, St Mary's Lane. The Standard had a Union Jack badge as its emblem. This model was first shown in the 1948 Motor Show when Austin launched its new A40 and the now forgotten Devon and Dorset motorcars were on display

1954. This was the view looking from the Fish Shambles up Little Eastgate towards the church. H. Pawson, the licensed horse slaughterer of Donnington-on-Bain, was still advertising his services, 'All animals painlessly destroyed', in this year.

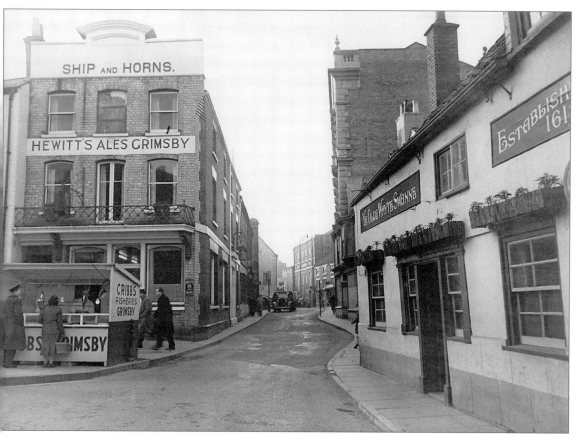

1954. Much thought was given to youth in the postwar years. This was a dance class photographed at Lacey Gardens. Children born in 1946/47 were known as bulge babies, after servicemen returned home.

1954. At the opposite end of the spectrum was the annual old people's tea at Legbourne. The Link, with its charitable works, was yet to come.

1954. This splendid selection of Christmas cakes was displayed at Louth County Hospital. Mr Hardy is on the far right.

This was the most original cake, modelled on the entrance to the Old Workshouse. Even in the '50s there was a certain stigma attached to Louth County Hospital, just because it had been the Old Workhouse!

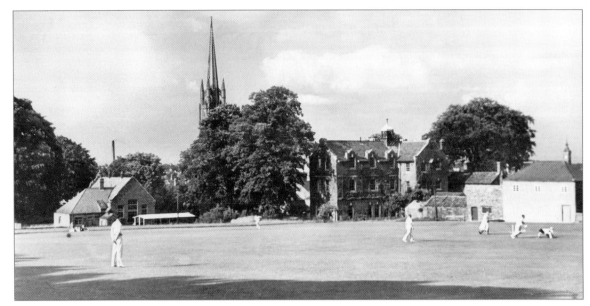

1955. The best cricket pitch in the Louth area could be found at King Edward VI Grammar School. On the reverse of this postcard its observant sender, with an acute sense of humour, wrote: 'This must be the dullest postcard of Louth ever! And reminds me horribly of the smell in the boys' locker rooms at school. How I detested it.'

1955. Louth 2nd XI cricket team waiting to go to an away match, photographed outside the Crown and Woolpack in the Cornmarket. From left to right: Mac Brown, Mick Lee, Cresswell Bonner George Charlton, Ernie Bosworth, Horace Dawson, Brian Papworth, -?-, Colin Johnson, Bert Bosworth (kneeling), Jack Casewell and John Barker. The photograph was taken by Bert Rawlings.

1955. Visiting speaker, John Eden MP, son of Sir Anthony Eden, photographed in Louth Town Hall. From left to right: Mrs Milligan-Manby, Mr Milligan-Manby, Sir Cyril Osborne, Henry Sharpley, -?-, Mrs Oscar Dixon, John Eden, Captain Helmer, Lady Osborne, Diana Dixon and Bill Dann. Sir Cyril Osborne split with the government over Suez.

1955. Apart from speeches, meetings and dances, there were also whist drives held in Louth Town Hall. Here we see some of the lucky winners with their prizes.

1955. During Louth Trade Fair in the Town Hall, Sir Cyril Osborne and his daughter, Jill Osborne, stop off at Sandwith's stand to view some choice products, while Mr Chris Sandwith (right) explains some of his merchandise. When Cyril Osborne was not working on parliamentary duties, he was a keen golfer. Charles Chappell was the Conservative agent in Louth.

1955. Mayor's Sunday saw Albert Ernest Maxey (five times Mayor of Louth) and Mr Holt, the Town Clerk, parading through Louth. Cyril Osborne MP and William Burr follow. This was the last time Maxey would be Mayor of Louth.

1955. A tea party was held at the Bowling Club to mark the ninetieth birthday of Thomas Robinson (1865–1963), seen here seated, centre, with walking stick and hat. Next to him is Mr Drinkel and, at the back, the familiar figure of Cecil Simpson, long-time curator of Louth Museum.

1956. The Lincolnshire Road Car Company staff party.

1956. An ecumenical meeting of different denominations gathered in Louth Museum for a meeting in July, chaired by Cyril Osborne MP.

Genteel times with afternoon tea and cucumber sandwiches in the rectory garden. The upheaval and aftermath of the Second World War encouraged such peaceful activities.

1955. In the '50s the institution of marriage was firmly entrenched and there were fewer divorces than today. This was the Plaskitt-Gray wedding.

1957. The name of Robinson is commonplace in Louth. This was Robinson's Stores at 14 Mercer Row, which had been established for over 100 years in Louth. It was the forerunner of what people would shortly call supermarkets. It should not be confused with Robinson's fruit and vegetable shop, which used to take pride of place in the old Market Hall.

1958. This photograph of Cordeaux School was taken on 25 July by Ken Atterby of the 'Owl' Studios, Northgate. Mr Stroud, centre, was Headmaster.

1959. With rock 'n' roll emerged a new generation of self-assured teenagers who would set the pattern for postwar Britain (see Introduction). Many of the teddy boys congregated around Frith's old café in the Market Place (currently on the site of New Look) where they would show off their bootlace ties, black suede shoes and three-quarter-length jackets with padded shoulders.

1959. Dances were held in the Pavilion at Louth Football Ground off Park Avenue in the '50s and '60s. Here we see a sprightly Mick Lee and Shirley Kendall rocking 'n' rolling.

On 6 March 1958 Alistair Grant was working as a farm labourer doing chores such as milking and mucking out cows on a dairy farm situated where Mr and Mrs Garside's house stands today, off Horncastle Road. He was paid the princely sum of £6 a week but it was one of the happiest times of his life. The rugby-loving Alistair Grant (1937–2001) pictured here posing as a modern executive, joined Batchelor Foods, then Fine Fare, before becoming MD of Safeway Supermarkets and eventually Chairman of the Argyll Group and Governor of the Bank of Scotland. He was knighted for his services.

1960. The staff and pupils of King Edward VI Grammar School. On either side of the bespectacled Mr Whitney (centre) are, left: Foster, Parkinson, Truner, Burley, -?-, Tether and Hobbs; and right: Hemming, Rowland, Mead, Braban, -?-, Benton, Rodgerson and Cooper. The quad is in the background.

The most famous old boy of King Edward VI Grammar School was Alfred, Lord Tennyson, a pupil from 1816 to 1820.

L. LOUTH.

This giant sycamore tree, known locally for as long as anyone can remember as Tennyson's tree, was cut down for safety reasons in 2001.

1959. Mr Neale's class, centre, at King Edward VI Grammar School. On Mr Neale's left are Dunn, Jenkinson, Rushbury and Towle. Sitting in the front row, far left, is Christopher 'Chris' Wright of Grimoldby, who later became a multi-millionaire with his Chrysalis record label.

1960. The Crown and Woolpack snooker team, which won the Snooker League. From left to right: -?-, Ron Taylor, Bob Cobb, Mick Lee, Tony West, Ray Parton (landlord), Byron Cook and Alan Brown.

1959 saw the death of George M. Hall (no relation to Maurice Hall). Most of his working life was spent working for Mawer Brothers (the builders and stone masons of Kidgate and Pawnshop Passage) but on his retirement he enjoyed repairing clocks. The one seen here was a Swiss clock with a trumpeter appearing on the hour instead of the usual cuckoo.

Left: 1961. Maurice Hall and Sir Herbert Broadley were awarded the Freedom of Louth. Together with R.A.F. Manby and Alderman Maxey, they were the only people to have had this honour bestowed upon them in the twentieth century. Maurice Hall, centre, wearing glasses, served Louth Town Council for thirty years.

Just as Louth had its own football team so did the outlying villages. This was the Grimoldby football team of 1961. Back row, left to right: Eric Willoughby, Bob Garbutt, John Lowry, George Vickers, Don Odlin, Mick Lee, 'Lofty' Harrison, Ian Wheatley. Front row: Brian Evison, Graham Lowry, Gordon Marshall, Barry Willerton and Jim Waumsley.

1961. This was Mr Rowland's class at King Edward VI Grammar School. Back row, far right: Bushell and Godfrey. Second row, left to right: Dunn, Hobson, Kingswood and N. Mawer. Front row: Jenkinson (whose father ran the Masons' Arms pub), Simpson, -?-, Mr Rowland, Baker, Jacques and Chris Wright. Geoffrey Baker later became Deputy Head of Lacey Gardens in Louth and wrote numerous children's books. His series of *Maurice* books was illustrated by Rolf Harris.

1961. One of the highlights of the year for these boys from King Edward VI Grammar School was a visit to the Houses of Parliament. Far left: Captain Ron Benton. Right: Mr Rowland. Centre: local MP Cyril Osborne, who showed the boys round.

1961. Laundry ladies at Louth County Hospital. These were the days before centralisation when each hospital was responsible for its own laundry. Second from left is Mrs Oliver and second from right Mrs Roberts.

Aerial view of High Holme Road, Newbridge Hill and Ramsgate shows the newly formed Lin Pac's works (centre). The site had previously been used by the Louth Arota works and by a canning factory. Louth station is still in use and East Lincs. Garages occupy the site of what was to become a Gateway/Somerfield supermarket.

1962. Here are two views of the interior of the Crown and Woolpack pub off the Cornmarket. In this one are two reporters, Paul from the *Louth Standard* and George Grammer from the *Evening Telegraph*. In the background is Ray Parton, landlord, and to the right a young Mick Lee. George Grammer went on to work for the *Daily Mirror*.

In this photograph an absorbing game of dominoes is taking place. The two gentlemen on the left are John Ranshaw and Tony Tilling.

In 1962 Eve and Ranshaw staged one of its many fashion shows. From left to right: Mrs Bunty Hersey (later Cockin), Joyce Munslow, Peggy Grant, Mary Mountain, Pat Taylor (later Little), Pat Clapp, Miss Oldridge, Mrs Joan Kenney and Eric Vamplew (proprietor of Eve and Ranshaw's).

1963. Saltfleet Manor opened its doors to the public on 5 July. Hobson Bocock's 2*d* guide of 1909 noted the Manor's Cromwellian relics, old English furniture, paintings and a window scratched with the names of Robert Fox and Jane Harvey. Robert Fox was a relative of John Foxe, who wrote the famous *Book of Martyrs*.

On 17 December 1966 the guest speaker at Louth's King Edward VI Grammar School was former pupil, Andrew Faulds MP. Before becoming Labour MP for Smethwick, the actor appeared in many historical film dramas including the classic *Jason and the Argonauts* and, as Jet Morgan, in the now legendary radio series *Journey into Space*. Andrew Faulds (1923–2000) was in Hawks House and is best remembered for carving 'Beer is Best' on one of the wooden pews in Eastgate Union church.

In November 1967 the once familiar landmark, the iron bridge spanning the Grimsby Road, was demolished after a tipping lorry crashed into it. This photograph shows young Brenda Sandwith standing to one side of the remains. The lorry responsible for the accident can clearly be seen with its tipping mechanism in the upright position.

4

To the Millennium

1981. Judging the Lovely Louth Competition are 'Sparks' Clarke, Margaret Needham, Grace Bett (well known for her flower arrangements) and George Cuppleditch. The photograph was taken on 13 July outside the Crown and Woolpack in New Street.

Left: 1974. One casualty from the demolition of large country houses in the postwar period was Eastfield Lodge. The similarity between this detail and the tower in George Street suggests that the same architect was responsible for both. *Below*: This view of Upgate typifies many of the changes that took place in postwar Louth. The Blue Stone Inn (to the left of this photo) was to be demolished. The old Black Bull would become an optician's and the Lincolnshire Gun Shop (once the Horse and Jockey) would shortly be converted into an Indian restaurant.

In the 1974 reorganisation of local government the old borough system disappeared, only to be replaced by the new Rural Urban District Council. Percy Fell was the first Mayor under the new regime (pictured here with Mrs Lilly Fell).

1974 saw Jeffrey Archer's resignation as MP for Louth. He went on to become a best-selling author, with his first novel *Not a Penny More, Not a Penny Less*, but returned to Lincolnshire many years later as inmate of North Sea Prison Camp, just north of Boston.

1976. Anthony Dixon, son of Lieutenant Colonel Oscar Dixon, was part of the Dixon family who owned the famous paper mill at West Marsh, Grimsby. The Dixon mill, responsible for Dixcel and Bronco toilet paper amongst other things, was sold to Bowater-Scott in 1972. Meanwhile, Anthony Dixon became High Steward of Louth (a post he held for a number of years) and President of the Louth Naturalists, Antiquarian and Literary Society. He is seen here opening the Link Day Centre on 25 September in the company of Mayor Stan Ward (left) and Mrs Roosevelt Wilkinson.

1977. Mayor Gladys Pacey Wilcox unveiling a plaque on the side of the Methodist chapel at the corner of Little Eastgate and Nicol Hill, to mark its rebuilding on 28 May. Mr and Mrs Stan Ward are on the right of the picture.

1978. The Conservative Annual Ball was held on 17 November in the Town Hall. Mr Michael Brotherton MP and Mrs Brotherton are on the far right, George Arliss (Mayor of Louth, 1980), centre, Mary Mountain MBE and Mr and Mrs Cuppleditch on the left. Jean Blackburn, the Conservative agent, is third from left.

15 February 1978. Louth has produced many fine coach-building firms, especially at the turn of the twentieth century. Chiefly centred around the Lud, off Chequergate, they manufactured thousands of carriages. Here we see a group of people inspecting an old conveyance. A youthful Peter Mountain is standing on the far right of the group.

By comparison, this was one of Louth's most prestigious carriages in use in the nineteenth century. The photograph was probably taken off Queen Street. The carriers' name was Hasewood.

1979. An extension was built on to St Margaret's Nursing Home on Victoria Road and opened by the Mayor. The Wolds family later turned this into the Beaumont Hotel.

After its conversion, many Louth firms and businesses had their Christmas parties at the Beaumont, and Norman Lamont was once seen escorting his mother to dinner here. Here is the *Grimsby Evening Telegraph* Christmas bash of 1992! Diane Butterfield (far left, next to Jacquie Ryan), Pat Laughton (second right) and Margaret Thomas (far right).

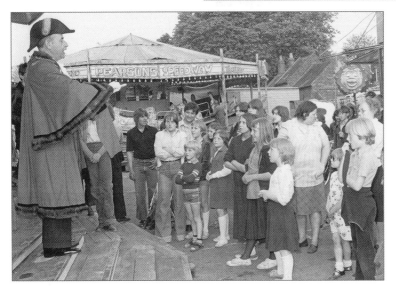

1979. One mayoral duty was to proclaim the opening of Louth's May Fair. Here we see Mayor George Cuppleditch performing his duty on 15 May in the Northgate car park. The photograph was taken by Ken Atterby.

1979. A feature of twentieth-century Louth was the South Wold Hunt. Despite many protests, the South Wold continues to meet on Boxing Day. This photograph shows Brian Dobson leading with Robin Godsmark on his left and Mike Vincent in the background together with other hunt enthusiasts.

The huntin', shootin' and fishin' fraternity has always been healthy in Lincolnshire. 1982 saw the arrival of yet another member to join the illustrious band, when William Haggas of Walmsgate Estates arrived in Louth. He is pictured with Lois the dog.

1981. At the junction of Eve Street with Northgate stood the old Primitive Methodist chapel –
on the site of Louth's current library. For years the building was used by Pickford's removals
and warehousing company.

1982. A meeting of speakers in Louth Town Hall on 20 November in front of Brown's famous
panoramic views of Louth. Back row, left to right: Lin Matthews, Sue Coote, the Revd David
Lambert and Lucy Hough. Front row: Mr Hough (Labour), Mrs Eleanor Bennett
(chairwoman), Mr John Sellick and Jill Brodie. The subject in question was Louth County
Hospital, a constant cause for concern.

24 March 1982. Louth Male Voice
Choir and members of Albatros pictured
during a civic reception at Louth Town
Hall. The Dutch choir Albatros, from
Nieuwe Pekela, has been a regular
favourite with Louth. From left to right:
Director of Music, Mr Anton Stulp,
Malcolm Neal, Mr G. De Wijh, Ray
Harniess, Don Harniess, Mr Hiebo Sagel
and David Bryant.

Many well known TV personalities
have visted Louth. Here we see
Su Pollard (star of *Hi-De-Hi*) passing
through on her way to visit her parents
at Sutton-on-Sea. The gentleman
pushing the trolley is Mr Harrison,
long-time employee of East Lindsay.
The photograph was taken outside the
Co-op (Pioneer) supermarket off
Northgate.

1982. The bridge at the bottom of Grimsby Road suffered a battering in December of this year when a lorry smashed into the parapet. The Bridge Street bridge had last undergone repairs after the 1920 flood.

Billy Platt's grocery shop finally closed its doors to the public. It had operated for over one hundred years as a provisions merchants, Mr Howson (Bill Platt's great-uncle) having started the business in 1883. Latterly a careless decorator removed the exterior shop sign and replaced it upside down, a tradition that Parker's, the present owners, continue.

1982 saw the death of Joan Mack (formerly Dobson), seen here on her wedding day. She married Robert Mack (1917–94), architect and founder member of Louth Rotary. Their son became one of the directors of Christian Salvesen.

1986. A Hawaiian evening at Thorpe Hall. Among the familiar faces past and present are Mr and Mrs Robin Mitchell (centre). One of the ancient traditions attached to this fine old house is the Thorpe Hall pew in St James's Church, which is permanently reserved for residents of the Hall.

Louth cricket team photographed at Scunthorpe. Back row, left to right: Peter Mountain, Mark Fisher, Terry Vamplew, Phil Johnson, Kevin Adlard, Terry Goodyear. Front row: Ian Patchett, -?-, Nick Mellows, Jeff Sardeson, David Bradley.

1987. Snooker champion Joe Johnson (left) visited Louth.

1986. Mayor Connie Jardine handing out Duke of Edinburgh awards in Louth Town Hall. Julie Everitt, in the floral dress, currently of Bridge McFarland, stands second from right next to Neal Malkin.

1986. A twinning gathering in Stainesway, Louth. The town twinned with its French counterpart, La Ferté-Bernard, near Le Mans in 1983. Pictured, left to right: Mrs Haydee Pheby, Jean Botras, -?-, -?-, Mike Pheby, Nesta Roberts, Jean Marwood, Ron Marwood, Norman Abell, -?-, Mary Abell.

1987. On 21 May the Duchess of Gloucester opened Smilies Clubhouse off St Bernard's Avenue. She is seen here (right) in the company of Pat Fowler from East Lindsey District Council.

1988. Young Sarah Kohut presented HRH Princess Anne with a bouquet when she officially opened the Livestock Centre at Louth cattle market.

Crowds of people waving banners and Union Jacks gathered to catch a glimpse of the Princess Royal.

1990. Shortly after its closure the Hat Box at 19 Upgate looked forlorn. It had a unique reputation throughout the county, but in the postwar period millinery became less and less fashionable.

1990. 'Remember, remember the fifth of November!' Bonfire night had become something of a feature in Louth at this time, with the biggest display being at Deighton Close. Here we see Phil Stevens, Derek Blow (Manager of Peacock and Binningtons), the Mayor, Joyce Munslow and David Williams of Rotary. Rotary and Louth Lions combined to stage this popular event.

1991. Patrick McLoughlin MP, Parliamentary Under-Secretary of State for Transport, officially opened Louth's long-awaited bypass. To accompany the event on 28 August there was a display of tractors, lorries, donkey rides and a parachute drop.

14 October 1991. 'Hello, Hello, Hello. What's all this then?' Zee German policemen in Louth? From left to right: Ray Bezant, a Lincoln traffic policeman, Dick Bolland, two German policemen, Roy Hobson and two more visiting German policemen.

2 March 1991. Overseeing the celebrations to mark the 150th year of Kidgate School are PC Sharp (senior) and PC Sharp (junior). The children wore costumes of a bygone era.

1991. Roy Gathercole opening a Fun Day at the Lincolnshire Poacher on 2 September.

1992. Kenneth Clarke MP during a visit to Louth on 6 November. From left to right: Air Commodore Jefferies, Peter Moran, Daphne Mitchell-Smith, Sir Peter Tapsell, Lady Gabrielle Tapsell, Phyllis West, Julia Barow, Kenneth Clarke, -?-, Dick Edington, Angela Edington. It has always surprised the author that Phyllis West has never received due recognition for her services to charity.

1992. Remembrance Day at the War Memorial, with Mayor David Shepherd and Mrs Shepherd in attendance. Also present were Town Clerk Weir and seven former Mayors of Louth: Dorothy Grant (1991), Roy Gathercole (1987), John Macdonald (1988), -?-, Magaret Ottoway (1996), John Dean (1993) and Clive Finch (1994). On the far left is the Mayor's Sergeant, Mr Cooper.

1993. Saving Ceres. The once familiar figure that stood in a niche on the old Corn Exchange was preserved after the building was demolished. Ceres (the Roman name for Demeter) was goddess of the earth's fruits and corn in particular. She currently resides to the side of Louth Town Hall.

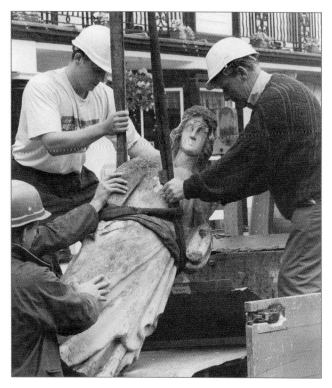

Left: Louth Playgoers Society's production of *Lettice and Lovage*, with, from left to right, Angela Davies, Christine (Chris Vickers), Patrick Carnworth and Glenna Betteridge, photo-graphed on 19 April. The Eton-educated Patrick Carnworth, whose brother is a High Court Judge, was suited to the boards – a local journalist by profession, with an emphasis on humour.

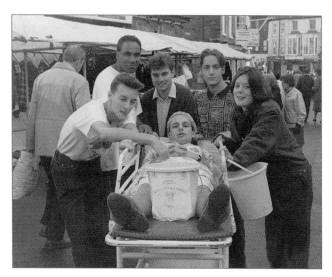

1992. On 2 November a group of King Edward VI pupils collect money for charity using this unusual vehicle, under the supervision of Mr Avtar Bath.

One of the highlights of the 1992 Louth Festival was a performance by Evelyn Glennie, the deaf percussionist, photographed in St James's Church. The event was the brainchild of Charles Baron and echoed shades of the Louth Eisteddfod, which took place back in the '20s.

1993. Popular novelist Helen Forrester photographed in the Conoco Rooms, signing copies of her books.

1994. Annie Topliss, author of *Music We Must Have*, receives a bouquet from Louth Choral Society's Vice-Chairman, Brian Wood, after serving for eleven years as Louth Choral Society's accompanist.

1994. The Kidgate summer fête this year was opened on 2 July by BBC TV children's presenter, Simon Parkin. For three hours he entertained the children with a series of games made famous in *Crackerjack*, the TV Broom Cupboard and Edd the Duck! One of his helpers was Morris dancer John Barter.

1994. Fun Day in Jubilee Crescent took place on 3 July, when four locals were photographed 'Dancing in the Streets'. Many people took part and danced the afternoon away.

1995. BBC's *Songs of Praise* was televised from St James's Church, Louth. Here we see part of the filming that took place on 7 September.

1995. One of the most successful Louth projects in the postwar period has been the renovation of Louth Canal by the Louth Navigation Trust. Here we see an unusual way of raising money by playing boule (or pétanque) at Ticklepenny Lock. Motorcycle ace Lee Brocklebank opened the event, while Malcolm Beaumont (dressed up in French beret and holding two boules) looks on.

Commemorating VE Day in Scarfe's Wine Bar. Rita (with Union Jack), Paul Hindley (right) and Robin Scarfe (centre) enjoyed an all-day party. (Scarfe's Wine Bar is now known as Kai's Bar – see page 31.)

1996. When Princess Alexandra came to open the new wing of Louth Hospital on 9 May, young Sarah Garrison presented her with a posy.

28 June 1996. The Duke of Gloucester opens Louth's new police station, off Eastfield Road.

1996. Louth's old police station to the right and Louth Magistrates Court to the left. The building in between has been demolished to make way for housing. Perhaps we will see Mr Caine's history of Louth Police Force in print one day.

1997. Footballer Emlyn Hughes takes time off to sign an autograph for two fans. Emlyn Hughes laid the foundation stone at the Sense project for young deaf-blind children in Old Mill Park in February 1992.

1997. Another well-known face, Hunter, from the successful television series *Gladiator*. Photographed at Manby on 29 May.

1997. Louth Dolphins at Louth swimming pool, opened by Dr Mary Archer, wife of Lord Archer, on 23 March 1974. The Dolphins were formed in 1986 and their present coach is Irene Arliss. Kate Haywood, aged fourteen, is an Olympic hopeful.

Aerial views of St James's. A comparison of these photographs clearly shows the in-filling and expansion that took place between *c.* 1924 (above) and 1998 (below).

1999. Sadly 23 September saw the untimely death of Susan (Sue) Grace Grant of Little Cawthorpe Manor. Just as Thorpe Hall has its legend of the Green Lady (a ghostly spectre which appears intermittently), so Cawthorpe Manor has its curse: the Mottram family, one of the former occupiers of the Manor, was wiped out by smallpox; a recusant priest starved to death in the priest hole; and Sue was the latest unfortunate victim. Her sparkle irradiated a wealth of splendour at Little Cawthorpe Manor.

The end of the Louth Gentlemen's Club was announced on 24 February 2000. Once, this fine old institution that began life in 1887, enjoyed a healthy membership. It held its final club dinner at the Masons' Arms on 20 April 2000. This photograph (from an earlier event in May 1995) shows some members and guests, including, left to right, Martin Chatterton, Richard Lake, Richard Potter, John Addison, Jim Laverack, Jonathan Humphries, Derek Green and James Laverack. The picture was taken by Ian Holmes.

2000. To celebrate the millennium, Louth Town Council produced an edition of bone china mugs emblazoned with the town crest to be given to every child of school age in Louth. Seen here are Mayor David Skinner (1999–2000) with Brian Hodgkinson (Mayor 2001–2002) and children showing off their commemorative memorabilia.

2000. Mayor John Dean (2000–1) and Lady Mayoress Christine Dean surrounded by immediate family, friends, fellow councillors and dignitaries as they gather for a photograph on the steps of Louth Town Hall.

2000. On 13 June members of the Louth branch of the Brigade of Guards gathered together for a reunion at Kenwick Hall.

Karl Blanch, a great fan of Louth's own Corinne Drewery of Swing Out Sister fame. Miss Drewery was educated at Cordeaux High School and her mother Elaine still resides at Authorpe, where she administers to hedgehogs at the Tiggywinkle Hedgehog Hospital.

In his guise as John Shuttleworth, Graham Fellows has delighted audiences with his alternative humour and, with his 'Jilted John' hit ('Gordon is a Moron'), he is a revered figure in pop history.

Revellers celebrating Louth millennium festivities in Cornmarket. From left to right: Noel Randall, the author, Sally Cuppleditch, Theodora Keightly, Sheila Keightly, John Keightly and Bev Randall with Albert Pearson.

List of Louth Members of Parliament
1892–2002

Sir Robert Perks	1892–1910	Lib
Captain Langton Brackenbury	1910; 1918–20	Con
Timothy Davies	1910–18	Lib
Thomas Wintringham	1920–1	Lib
Margaret Wintringham	1921–4	Lib
Lieutenant Colonel Sir Arthur Heneage	1924–45	Con
Sir Cyril Osborne	1945–69	Con
Jeffrey Archer	1969–74	Con
Michael Brotherton	1974–83	Con
Sir Peter Tapsell	1983–	Con (E. Lindsey)

ACKNOWLEDGEMENTS

In preparing this book I am extremely grateful to the following: C.C. Pond (House of Commons Library), Henry Sharpley, Tim Dixon, Sue Jarnell, Peggy Grant, David Sandwith, Mick and Christine Lee, the late Brian Howe, David Williams, Maureen and Terry Vamplew, Peter Craig, Peter Chapman, Linda Roberts, Peter Moore (Editor, *Grimsby Evening Telegraph*), Geoffrey Baker and Richard and Margaret Needham, Adam Grist and Norman Abell.

Other books by David Cuppleditch

Around Louth
Boston
Postwar Lincoln
Lincolnshire Memories
Lincolnshire Wolds
Lincolnshire Coast
A Century of Grimsby
Lincoln: The Twentieth Century
Lincoln Cathedral
Hong Kong
The London Sketch Club